VEGETABLES

VEGETABLES

PERFECTLY PREPARED TO ENJOY EVERY DAY

This edition published in 2012
LOVE FOOD is an imprint of Parragon Books Ltd

Parragon
Chartist House
15–17 Trim Street
Bath, BA1 1HA, UK

www.parragon.com/lovefood

ISBN: 978-1-78186-728-0

Printed in China

Concept: Patrik Jaros & Günter Beer
Recipes and food styling: Patrik Jaros www.foodlook.com
Text: Günter Beer, Gerhard von Richthofen, Patrik Jaros, Jörg Zipprick
Photography: Günter Beer www.beerfoto.com
Photographer's assistants: Sigurd Buchberger, Aranxa Alvarez
Cook's assistants: Magnus Thelen, Johannes von Bemberg
Designed by Estudio Merino www.estudiomerino.com
Produced by Buenavista Studio s.l. www.buenavistastudio.com
The visual index is a registered design of Buenavista Studio s.l. (European Trademark
Office number 000252796-001)
Project management: trans texas publishing, Cologne
Typesetting: Nazire Ergün, Cologne

Notes for the Reader
This book uses standard kitchen measuring spoons and cups. All spoon and cup measurements are
level unless otherwise indicated. Unless otherwise stated, milk is assumed to be whole, butter is
assumed to be salted, eggs are large, individual vegetables are medium, and pepper is freshly ground
black pepper. Unless otherwise stated, all root vegetables should be washed and peeled before using.

Garnishes and serving suggestions are all optional and not necessarily included in the recipe
ingredients or method. The times given are only an approximate guide. Preparation times differ
according to the techniques used by different people and the cooking times may also vary from
those given. Optional ingredients, variations, or serving suggestions have not been included in
the calculations.

Recipes using raw or very lightly cooked eggs should be avoided by infants, the elderly, pregnant
women, and people with weakened immune systems. Pregnant and breast-feeding women are advised
to avoid eating peanuts and peanut products. People with nut allergies should be aware that some
of the prepared ingredients used in the recipes in this book may contain nuts. Always check the
packaging before use.

Picture acknowledgments
All photos by Günter Beer, Barcelona

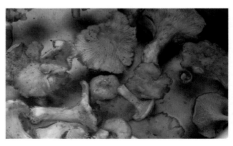

Contents

Introduction

Fresh, flavorsome vegetables are a key part of a healthy, balanced diet. They contain numerous vitamins and minerals, are rich in fiber, and are virtually fat-free. Vegetables are also one of the most versatile of foods and can be prepared in a multitude of ways. They taste good boiled, fried, roasted, steamed, and raw.

Buy vegetables when they are in season, because this is when they are especially fresh and nutritious. However, vegetables that are quickly frozen immediately after harvesting are a good alternative to fresh produce. It's always best to buy smaller quantities and avoid storing vegetables for too long, because only fresh vegetables are really full of flavor. It's also important not to peel or cut up vegetables too far in advance before they are cooked, because they lose important nutrients when exposed to air or soaked in water. Many types of vegetables have the highest concentration of vitamins immediately under their skin, so try to remove as little of this as possible. A vegetable peeler is a worthwhile investment.

Different vegetables can be cooked in different ways. Tougher root vegetables, for example, require longer than the more sensitive stem vegetables. Some types of vegetables are best al dente, while others should be cooked thoroughly. The chart on page 9 gives a basic overview of recommended cooking times for individual types of vegetables.

Vegetables are divided into groups according to common characteristics. These are the most important categories:

"Fruit" vegetables
This category includes tomatoes, bell peppers, eggplants, avocados, cucumbers, pumpkins, and zucchini. From a botanical point of view, these types of vegetables are actually fruit because they bear the plant's seeds. However, they are usually prepared like vegetables, as savory dishes. These vegetables are rich in vitamins, minerals, and fiber and are characterized by their bright colors, which give dishes their wonderful appearance. When buying these vegetables, make sure they are ripe but firm and the skin is intact. They can be sautéed, steamed, roasted, or stewed. Cucumbers, tomatoes, bell peppers, and avocados are traditional salad ingredients and can also be eaten raw, as can zucchini.

Leafy vegetables
This category includes lettuce, spinach, kale, Swiss chard, and frisée. Rinse leafy vegetables well under running water before preparation to remove any residual soil or sand. When you buy this type of vegetable, make sure the leaves have not turned yellow or brown and do not look limp. Use leafy vegetables as soon as possible after purchase, and do not keep them in the refrigerator for more than two days. When planning a meal, remember that leafy vegetables collapse when cooked, so that only a small volume will be left. These vegetables cook relatively quickly and can be sautéed, stir-fried, boiled, or eaten raw in salads.

Legumes
This category includes beans, lentils, and peas. Legumes are rich in protein, carbohydrates, minerals, and fiber and are an excellent basis for numerous dishes, especially vegetarian ones. Fresh beans and peas can be cooked briefly in boiling water or stir-fried. Soak dried beans overnight or for at leat five hours, then drain and rinse before preparing.

Brassicas
These vegetables are in the cabbage family, including green cabbage, red cabbage, cauliflower, broccoli, bok choy, Brussels sprouts, arugula, napa cabbage, and kohlrabi. They are all great sources of vitamins, minerals, and fiber. When buying these vegetables, make sure the leaves are not bruised or marked. They usually have an intense aroma, which gets

stronger the longer they are cooked. Do not overcook any of the brassica family, or they will be unappetizing. When these vegetables are young and fresh, they can be used successfully in salads, tossed in a flavorful dressing.

Bulb vegetables

This category includes onions, shallots, garlic, scallions, leeks, and chives. Bulb vegetables have a pungent aroma and add a strong flavor to many dishes. When buying bulb vegetables, make sure the outer skin of onions, shallots, and garlic is dry and that no shoots (which can give the bulb a bitter flavor) have developed. Leeks and scallions should always have white tips and lush green leaves that

should never look limp. Bulb vegetables can be used as the basis of a variety of dishes, such as soups, stews, and casseroles, and they can be sautéed for serving as a side dish or even be fried to create a crisp garnish.

Stem vegetables

This category includes asparagus, fennel, celery, and artichokes. These vegetables need to be cooked for very different lengths of time. Make sure the vegetables are not discolored and that they feel firm when purchased. Stem vegetables can be boiled, steamed, sautéed, or stewed, and they also taste delicious when roasted in the oven. Some can also be used raw in salads.

Root and tuber vegetables

This category of vegetables, which grow underground, includes potatoes, carrots, celeriac, parsnips, turnips, and beets. These traditional winter vegetables are popular and are among the most varied in terms of flavor. Root vegetables add substance and flavor to comforting soups, stews, and roasts. They are full of vitamins and are a good source of carbohydrates, which supply the body with necessary energy. You should buy only firm vegetables that are not discolored. Root vegetables have a crunchy consistency and develop a pleasantly sweet flavor when cooked. They can be steamed, boiled, stewed, and roasted in the oven.

How to use this book

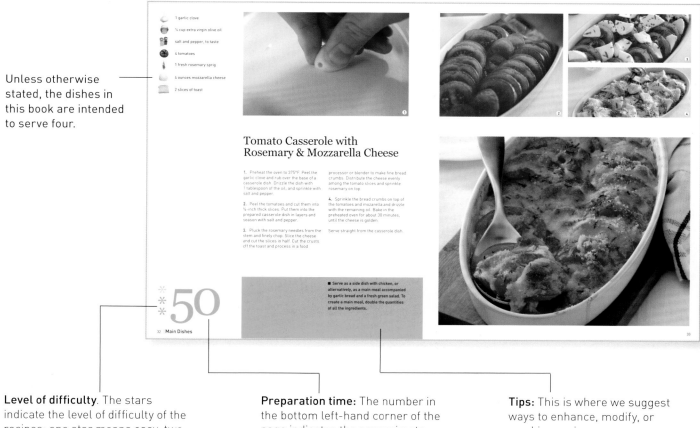

Unless otherwise stated, the dishes in this book are intended to serve four.

Level of difficulty. The stars indicate the level of difficulty of the recipes: one star means easy, two intermediate, three difficult.

Preparation time: The number in the bottom left-hand corner of the page indicates the approximate preparation time in minutes.

Tips: This is where we suggest ways to enhance, modify, or combine recipes.

Vegetable Cuts

Batons: Broad strips, approximately ½ inch wide and 2 inches long, are used as a garnish for sauces and also as an accompaniment to poached fish dishes.

Julienne: Thin vegetable strips that are approximately ⅛ inch thick and 2–2¾ inches long, they are suitable for potato dishes, for poaching with fish, or as a garnish for soups and sauces.

Brunoise: Delicate ⅛-inch cubes that are used for salad dressings, as a garnish for fish sauces, for dishes with beans and lentils, and for stews. They can also be poached with whole vegetables.

Small dice: These ¼-inch cubes are suitable for soups and stews, and they cook in approximately 15 minutes.

Medium dice: These ½-inch cubes are suitable ingredients for sauces that are not cooked for too long. Ratatouille ingredients can also be diced in this manner, as well as vegetables for rustic soups and stews.

Large dice: At approximately ¾–1¼-inches, these cubes are suitable for braising with roasts and stews or gently sautéing and adding to gravies.

Soup vegetables: refers to vegetables that are simply cut into quarters or thirds. They are added to soups or stocks that have to cook for a long time, and they don't cook down as fast as the other vegetable cuts.

Small mirepoix: Cut the vegetables into medium cubes. Cut unpeeled garlic cloves in half. Use 2 parts of onions to each 1 part of the other root vegetables (celery, carrots, celeriac, or parsley root). Small mirepoix is used as an addition to shellfish and poultry sauces.

Large mirepoix: Peel the vegetables and cut them into coarse pieces or cubes measuring about 1¼ inches. Cut unpeeled garlic cloves in half. The same proportions of vegetables are used for both small and large mirepoix. Large mirepoix is used for meat sauces or vegetable stocks, or in marinades for game.

Cooking Chart

Product	Form	Method	Temperature	Time
Artichokes	Whole	In water	Boiling	35 minutes
Artichokes	Slices	Skillet	Medium heat	8 minutes
Artichokes	Quarters	Skillet	Medium heat	12 minutes
Asparagus, green	Whole	In water	Boiling	6 minutes
Asparagus, green	Pieces	Skillet	Medium heat	5 minutes
Asparagus, white	Pieces	Skillet	Medium heat	8 minutes
Asparagus, white	Whole	In water	Boiling	10 minutes
Bell peppers	Batons	Skillet	Medium heat	10 minutes
Bell peppers	Small dice	Skillet	Medium heat	3 minutes
Broccoli	Florets	Skillet	Medium heat	15 minutes
Broccoli	Whole	In water	Boiling	20 minutes
Button mushrooms	Slices	Skillet	High heat	4 minutes
Cabbage	Quarters	Oven	325°F	45 minutes
Cabbage	Slices	Saucepan with lid	Medium heat	35 minutes
Cabbage	Slices	Skillet	High heat	10 minutes
Carrots	Julienne strips	In water	Boiling	10 minutes
Carrots	Slices	Skillet	Medium heat	6 minutes
Carrots	Small dice	In water	Boiling	8 minutes
Cauliflower	Whole	In water	Boiling	25 minutes
Cauliflower	Florets	Skillet	Medium heat	15 minutes
Chanterelles	Whole	Skillet	High heat	3 minutes
Cucumber	Slices	Skillet	Medium heat	6 minutes
Cucumber	Whole	Oven	325°F	20 minutes
Eggplants	Large dice	Skillet	Medium heat	8 minutes
Fava beans	Whole	In water	Boiling	2 minutes
Fennel	Batons	Skillet	Medium heat	2 minutes
Fennel	Small dice	Skillet	Medium heat	1 minute
Green beans	Whole	In water	Boiling	2 minutes
Leeks	Julienne strips	Skillet	Medium heat	1 minute
Leeks	Slices	Skillet	Medium heat	2 minutes
Leeks	In thirds or quarters	In water	Boiling	20 minutes
Morel mushrooms	Whole	Skillet	Medium heat	6 minutes
Pea pods	Whole	Skillet	Medium heat	1 minute
Peas	Shelled	In water	Boiling	2 minutes
Porcini mushrooms	Slices	Skillet	High heat	5 minutes
Spinach	Whole	Skillet	Medium heat	5 minutes
Swiss chard	Leaf	Skillet	Medium heat	5 minutes
Swiss chard	Stalk	Skillet	Medium heat	8 minutes
Tomatoes	Small dice	Skillet	Medium heat	1 minute
Zucchini	Slices	Skillet	Medium heat	6 minutes
Zucchini	Julienne strips	In water	Boiling	8 minutes
Zucchini	Batons	In water	Boiling	10 minutes
Zucchini	Small dice	Skillet	Medium heat	8 minutes

3 small carrots

1 small leek

2 celery stalks

½ zucchini

2 scallions

8 cherry tomatoes

1 garlic clove

¼ cup olive oil

salt and pepper, to taste

½ teaspoon fennel seeds, crushed

6 cups vegetable stock

few fresh basil leaves, torn

1 teaspoon fresh oregano leaves

1 cup freshly grated
Parmesan cheese

Italian Vegetable Soup

1. Cut the carrots, leek, celery, zucchini, and scallions into ¼-inch pieces. Cut the tomatoes into quarters. Peel the garlic and finely dice.

2. Heat the oil in a large saucepan, add the garlic, and cook until lightly browned. Add the scallions and leek and sauté.

3. Add the carrots, celery, and zucchini and sauté without browning. Season with salt and pepper and add the crushed fennel seeds.

4. Add the tomatoes, pour in the stock, and gently simmer for about 10 minutes.

5. Add the basil and oregano to the soup.

Ladle into warm bowls and garnish with the cheese. Serve immediately.

40

■ If the garlic clove is already growing a green stem, remove it with a knife because it can taste bitter and sharp when cooked.

1 garlic clove

½ cup extra virgin olive oil

1 cucumber

2 red bell peppers

½ onion

3 cups tomato juice

salt and pepper, to taste

2 tablespoons red wine vinegar

Gazpacho

1. Peel the garlic clove, then press through a garlic crusher into ⅓ cup of the oil and stir. Set aside.

2. Coarsely peel the cucumber and cut into ¾-inch dice. Seed the red bell peppers and cut into ¾-inch dice. Cut the onion into ¾-inch dice.

3. Put the vegetables in a blender or food processor.

4. Pour in the tomato juice.

5. Season with salt and pepper, then add the vinegar and the remaining oil.

6. Puree for about 1 minute.

7. Pour into a bowl and chill in the refrigerator for at least 1 hour so the soup can cool completely.

Drizzle a little of the garlic oil over the soup shortly before serving. Place a tall container of crushed ice in the soup bowl, so the soup stays chilled once served..

*
* *70
*

■ During summer, you can use overripe, soft tomatoes instead of tomato juice.

2 scallions

 2 fresh flat-leaf parsley sprigs, plus extra to garnish

1 pound flat-cap mushrooms

1 garlic clove

3 tablespoons vegetable oil

salt and pepper, to taste

½ teaspoon caraway seeds

4 slices whole-wheat bread

Garlic-Caraway Fried Flat Mushrooms on Bread

1. Slice the scallions into rings. Finely chop the parsley.

2. Clean the mushrooms, remove the stems, and put the caps upside down into a skillet.

3. Finely chop the garlic. Pour the oil over the mushrooms, reserving 1 teaspoon, and cook them gently over medium heat.

4. Sprinkle the scallions, garlic, and parsley over the mushrooms and season with salt and pepper. Drizzle the remaining oil on the caraway seeds and chop them, then add them to the skillet.

Remove the mushrooms from the skillet with some of the oil and arrange on the slices of bread, garnished with parsley sprigs. Serve immediately.

■ Different types of mushrooms, such as cremini, oyster, or shiitake, can also be used for this recipe.

2¾ cups all-purpose flour

2 teaspoons baking powder

3 eggs

1¾ cups beer

⅓ cup vegetable oil

½ teaspoon salt

3 zucchini

4 fresh thyme sprigs

1 cup plain yogurt

juice of 1 lemon

salt and pepper, to taste

9 cups peanut oil

Zucchini in a Thyme Batter with Yogurt Sauce

1. Put the flour and the baking powder into a bowl and mix. Separate the eggs, then add the egg yolks to the flour. Slowly pour in the beer and mix with a wire whisk until a smooth batter forms. Stir in the vegetable oil. Beat the egg whites with the salt until holding soft peaks, then fold into the batter.

2. Cut the zucchini into ½-inch-thick slices. Pluck the thyme leaves from the stems and place them and the zucchini slices into the batter. Put the yogurt into a bowl, add the lemon juice, and season with salt and pepper. Stir the mixture until smooth.

3. Heat the peanut oil to 325°F in a wide saucepan, then add the zucchini slices and fry until golden on both sides. Drain on paper towels and lightly sprinkle with salt.

Serve the zucchini slices on a platter with the yogurt dip and a wedge of lemon.

40

■ The batter can also be prepared with white wine or mineral water instead of beer. Batter-coated fried basil or sage leaves make a delicious snack with an aperitif.

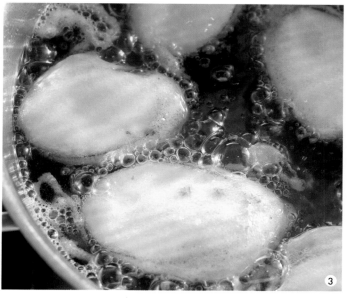

 ½ bunch fresh cilantro

1 orange

2 cups cooked millet

1 egg

½ cup light cream

2 tablespoons bread crumbs

salt, to taste

white pepper, to taste

2 tablespoons olive oil

Millet Cakes with Cilantro & Orange Zest

1. Coarsely chop the cilantro. Bring a small saucepan of lightly salted water to a boil. Using a vegetable peeler, peel off two strips of zest from the orange and add to the boiling water for 1 minute, to soften. Rinse the strips and cut them into thin slices. Cut the orange into slices and set aside.

2. Put the millet into a bowl. Add the egg, cream, and bread crumbs.

3. Add the orange zest and cilantro. Season with salt and pepper.

4. Carefully mix together the ingredients and, with moist hands, shape into small patties. Press them together well so they don't fall apart when sautéing.

5. Heat the oil in a skillet over medium heat, add the patties, and sauté on both sides until golden brown.

Transfer the cakes to plates and serve with salad greens and the reserved orange slices.

■ Couscous or quinoa can be used instead of millet. Grate the orange peel and add some fresh ginger to the mix, then shape the patties and sauté as described above.

8 ounces mixed ground beef, pork and lamb

1 cup coarsely crumbled goat cheese

1 egg

2 tablespoons bread crumbs

3 scallions, sliced into rings

1 tablespoon shredded fresh basil, plus extra sprigs to garnish

salt and pepper, to taste

1 teaspoon dried oregano

2 large eggplants

olive oil, for greasing

2 cups tomato juice

1 tablespoon sugar

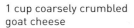

Stuffed Eggplants with Goat Cheese & Oregano

1. Preheat the oven to 350°F. Put the ground meat, cheese, egg, bread crumbs, scallion rings, and basil strips in a large bowl, season with salt and pepper, and add the oregano.

2. Mix the filling by hand. Do not knead it, because the pieces of cheese will need to be distinguishable in the finished dish.

3. Cut off the stems of the eggplants and cut them in half lengthwise. Trim off some of the curved bottom, so that they will be more stable.

4. Scoop out the inside of the eggplants with a spoon, coarsely dice the flesh, and gently combine with the meat mixture.

5. Generously grease a casserole dish with oil and put the eggplant halves into it. Fill them with the meat-and-cheese mixture and bake in the preheated oven for approximately 45 minutes. Add some water from time to time and baste the eggplants with the juice produced. Mix the tomato juice with the sugar, season with salt and pepper, and pour the juice over the eggplant halves. Bake for an additional 15 minutes.

Divide the eggplant halves among four warm plates, then pour some of the sauce around, garnish with basil, and serve immediately.

✳
✳
✳ **80**

■ You can make this recipe using zucchini, bell peppers, or cucumbers instead of eggplants.

1 onion

1 head cauliflower

½ bunch fresh cilantro

⅓ cup vegetable oil

1 teaspoon cumin seeds

6 star anise

salt and pepper, to taste

⅔ cup water

10–12 cherry tomatoes

Cauliflower with Tomatoes & Cumin

1. Finely chop the onion. Divide the cauliflower into small florets. Coarsely chop the cilantro.

2. Heat ¼ cup of the oil in a saucepan. Add the cumin seeds and the star anise and lightly brown, but do not cook them for too long, or the spices will burn and become bitter or lose some of their flavor.

3. Add the cauliflower and gently sauté for about 5 minutes. Season with salt and pepper, then add the water and cook for an additional 5 minutes, covered, until the liquid is reduced.

4. Add the tomatoes to the pan and gently sauté for 5 minutes. Heat the remaining oil in a skillet, then add the onion and cook until golden.

Arrange the cauliflower on plates, sprinkle with the onion and cilantro, and serve immediately.

■ Serve the spicy cauliflower with a cooling yogurt dip on the side. Instead of cauliflower, you can add a choice of broccoli, kohlrabi, or carrots. When prepared in this way, the vegetables taste nice and spicy, but also retain a crunchy texture.

1¼ pounds chanterelle mushrooms

2 shallots

3 tablespoons butter

salt and pepper, to taste

freshly grated nutmeg

½ bunch fresh parsley

1 cup light cream

2 tablespoons sour cream or crème fraîche

juice of 1 lemon

Mushroom Ragout with Nutmeg & Parsley

1. Clean the mushrooms and wash them in cold water. Do not let them become saturated. Drain well on paper towels.

2. Cut the large mushrooms into ¼-inch slices, leaving the small ones whole. Finely chop the shallots.

3. Melt the butter in a large saucepan, add the shallots, and gently sauté until they are translucent, stirring continuously with a wooden spoon.

4. Add the mushrooms, season with salt, pepper, and nutmeg, and sauté for an additional 2–3 minutes. Finely chop the parsley.

5. Add the cream and the sour cream and simmer for approximately 5 minutes, then add the lemon juice.

Mix in the parsley and serve immediately.

* * * 40

■ Other types of mushrooms, such as porcini, cremini, or wild mushrooms, can be prepared in the same way. You can also use a mix of different mushrooms, and serve with dumplings.

1 eggplant

1 large zucchini

1 onion

2 green bell peppers

1 red bell pepper

1 fennel bulb

4 garlic cloves

½ teaspoon fennel seeds

⅓ cup olive oil

3 fresh thyme sprigs

3 fresh rosemary sprigs

salt, to taste

1 bay leaf

pepper, to taste

1 (14½-ounce) can peeled tomatoes

1 fresh basil sprig, to garnish

Ratatouille

1. Cut all of the vegetables into ¾-inch cubes. Peel the garlic and finely chop. Prepare the fennel seeds by drizzling a little of the oil over them, then finely chop. Pluck the thyme leaves and the rosemary needles from their stems and coarsely chop. Heat the remaining oil in a large saucepan. Add the eggplant, season with salt, and sauté for about 5 minutes.

2. Push the eggplant to the side, add the garlic to the center of the pan, and gently sauté until golden brown.

3. Add the remaining vegetables to the center of the pan and gently sauté for about 2 minutes.

4. Add the bay leaf, thyme, rosemary, and fennel seeds. Mix well, season with salt and pepper and gently sauté for an additional 5 minutes.

5. Clear a space in the center of the pan, add the tomatoes, season with salt, and cook over low heat for an additional 15 minutes, stirring frequently so that the vegetables don't brown. Add a little water occasionally, if necessary.

Garnish the ratatouille with fresh basil leaves and serve warm or cold.

■ Combine the vegetables in different proportions to suit your tastes. Chop the vegetables into smaller, ¼-inch cubes to create a perfect accompaniment for pasta.

- 2 red bell peppers
- 1 green bell pepper
- 3 small onions
- 4 Yukon gold potatoes
- 2 garlic cloves
- rind of 1 lemon
- ½ teaspoon caraway seeds
- 3 tablespoons vegetable oil
- 2 teaspoons sweet paprika
- salt and pepper, to taste
- 5 cups vegetable stock

Vegetable Goulash

1. Halve, core, and seed the red bell peppers and the green bell pepper and cut them into ¾-inch pieces. Coarsely dice the onions. Peel the potatoes, cut them into ¾-inch pieces, and cover them with cold water to prevent discoloration. Peel the garlic cloves and finely chop with the lemon rind. Prepare the caraway seeds by drizzling a little of the oil on them and then chopping them.

2. Heat the remaining oil in a stainless steel saucepan, add the onions, and sauté. Drain the potato pieces in a colander. Add the potatoes to the onions and gently sauté for 5 minutes.

3. Sprinkle the garlic, lemon rind, caraway seeds, and paprika over the potatoes and onions and gently sauté.

4. Add the red bell peppers and green bell pepper to the pan, season with salt and pepper, and gently sauté over medium heat for a few minutes.

5. Pour in the stock and simmer for about 25 minutes, stirring occasionally.

Ladle the goulash into warm bowls and serve immediately with rye bread.

***55

■ Zucchini and whole cherry tomatoes can be used instead of green and red peppers, if preferred.

1²⁄₃ cups all-purpose flour, plus extra for dusting

1¼ sticks butter, chilled

salt, to taste

4 eggs

1 tablespoon water

3 leeks

4 ounces bacon strips

pepper, to taste

²⁄₃ cup light cream

freshly grated nutmeg

8 ounces Gruyère cheese or Swiss cheese

Quiche Lorraine with Leeks

1. Sift the flour onto a work surface. Work half of the butter and ½ teaspoon salt into the flour. Add 1 egg and the water and knead the mixture quickly into a smooth dough, so that the butter doesn't become too warm and the pastry doesn't puff up when baked. Cover in plastic wrap and chill in the refrigerator for 30 minutes. Invert the dough onto a lightly floured work surface and roll it out evenly with a rolling pin to a thickness of ⅛ inch. Dust with flour to prevent it from sticking to the work surface.

2. Place an oval tart pan on top of the rolled-out dough to check that it is large enough. Roll the dough around the rolling pin to lift.

3. Grease the tart pan with ½ tablespoon of the butter, then unroll the dough and fit it into the pan, making sure that it doesn't tear.

4. Press the dough into the edges of the pan and cut off the surplus projecting over the sides. Prick with a fork so that it doesn't puff up during baking. Put the dish in the refrigerator until it is needed.

5. Preheat the oven to 350°F. Slice the leeks into rings, wash them under cold running water, and drain well. Cut the bacon strips into small pieces. Add the remaining butter to a skillet and heat until foaming, add the bacon strips, and gently sauté, then add the leeks. Season the mixture with salt and pepper and

+ 30 minutes resting

45

■ Instead of leeks, you can use button mushrooms or oyster mushrooms. This quiche is also delicious with ratatouille or fennel bulb and red bell peppers.

continue to sauté for about 5 minutes, until the leeks have wilted and the liquid has reduced.

6. Whisk the cream with the remaining eggs in a small bowl seasoned with salt, pepper, and nutmeg. Finely shred the cheese and set aside.

7. Remove the tart pan from the refrigerator and spread the leek-bacon mixture evenly over the bottom.

8. Spread the shredded cheese over the top of the filling and cover it with the cream-egg mixture. Bake in the preheated oven for 15–20 minutes.

Let stand briefly, then cut the quiche into wedges and arrange them on plates to serve.

1 garlic clove

¼ cup extra virgin olive oil

salt and pepper, to taste

4 tomatoes

1 fresh rosemary sprig

4 ounces mozzarella cheese

2 slices of toast

Tomato Casserole with Rosemary & Mozzarella Cheese

1. Preheat the oven to 375°F. Peel the garlic clove and rub over the base of a casserole dish. Drizzle the dish with 1 tablespoon of the oil, and sprinkle with salt and pepper.

2. Peel the tomatoes and cut them into ¼-inch thick slices. Put them into the prepared casserole dish in layers and season with salt and pepper.

3. Pluck the rosemary needles from the stem and finely chop. Slice the cheese and cut the slices in half. Cut the crusts off the toast and process in a food processor or blender to make fine bread crumbs. Distribute the cheese evenly among the tomato slices and sprinkle rosemary on top.

4. Sprinkle the bread crumbs on top of the tomatoes and mozzarella and drizzle with the remaining oil. Bake in the preheated oven for about 30 minutes, until the cheese is golden.

Serve straight from the casserole dish.

* *
* **50**

■ Serve as a side dish with chicken, or alternatively, as a main meal accompanied by garlic bread and a fresh green salad. To create a main meal, double the quantities of all the ingredients.

8 carrots

2 celery stalks

2 ounces shallots

1¼ pounds of pumpkin, or butternut squash

1-inch piece fresh ginger

2 tablespoons butter

1¾ tablespoons olive oil

salt and pepper, to taste

1 teaspoon sweet paprika

pinch of curry powder

2 tablespoons ketchup

1 bay leaf

1 cup chicken stock

1 cup light cream

1 cup milk

freshly grated nutmeg

¾ cup shredded fontina cheese or Gruyère cheese

Pumpkin Casserole with Fontina Cheese & Paprika

1. Preheat the oven to 375°F. Chop the carrots, celery, and shallots into ¼-inch cubes, then chop the pumpkin into ¾-inch cubes. Peel and finely grate the ginger.

2. Add the butter and oil to a wide saucepan and heat until foaming. Add the shallots and sauté until translucent, then add the celery and carrots and sauté. Add the pumpkin, season with salt and pepper, then add the ginger, paprika, and curry powder and brown for 5 minutes.

3. Push the ingredients to the side of the pan and put the ketchup in the center. Lightly brown the ketchup and then mix it with the other ingredients.

4. Add the bay leaf and the stock. Simmer for about 5 minutes, stirring continuously. Add the cream and the milk and bring to a boil. Simmer gently for an additional 5 minutes.

5. Remove the bay leaf, season the pumpkin with nutmeg, and spread it evenly in the bottom of a casserole dish. Sprinkle the cheese over the pumpkin. Bake in the preheated oven for about 15 minutes. Cover the dish with aluminum foil if the cheese is browning too quickly.

Serve straight from the casserole dish.

■ The quantities specified above will serve two people.

16 red cherry tomatoes
on the vine

4 yellow cherry tomatoes
on the vine

1 pound tofu

½ bunch fresh Thai basil leaves

10–12 baby corn

2 tablespoons peanut oil

1 tablespoon packed
light brown sugar

1 teaspoon red curry paste

2½ cups coconut milk

3 tablespoons soy sauce

Tofu in Hot Curry Sauce with Thai Basil & Baby Corn

1. Remove the tomatoes from the vine. Cut the tofu into 1¼-inch cubes. Strip the Thai basil leaves from the stalks and set aside. Cut the baby corn in half lengthwise.

2. Heat the oil in a saucepan. Add the sugar and curry paste and heat until caramelized, then add the coconut milk. Add the soy sauce and simmer for an additional 3 minutes.

3. Add the tofu, tomatoes, and corn and simmer for an additional 3 minutes, stirring continuously.

4. Add the Thai basil leaves, reserving a few to garnish.

Serve the curry in bowls, garnished with the reserved Thai basil leaves.

* * * 25

■ For anyone who enjoys a fruitier curry, add fresh pineapple or mango cut into small cubes. You can also replace the Thai basil with fresh cilantro.

 ½ teaspoon red curry paste

2 tablespoons oyster sauce

8 ounces seitan

8 ounces green asparagus

1 head broccoli

3 tablespoons vegetable oil

Broccoli with Asparagus & Seitan

1. Place the curry paste in a small bowl, add the oyster sauce, and mix to make a marinade.

2. Cut the seitan into finger-size strips. Cut the woody ends off the asparagus and cut the spears into 2-inch pieces. Divide the broccoli into small florets.

3. Put the seitan into the marinade and set aside for about 15 minutes.

4. Heat the oil in a skillet. Add the broccoli and sauté, then add the asparagus pieces and sauté.

5. Add the marinated seitan strips and mix together well.

Serve in small bowls.

■ Seitan is made from gluten and is commonly used as a substitute for meat in vegetarian dishes. It is not widely available, but you can find it in health-food stores and specialty online stores.

- 1 pound potato gnocchi

- 1½ cups low-fat plain yogurt

- 2 teaspoons tandoori seasoning

- juice of ½ lemon

- salt and pepper, to taste

- 1 cup milk

- 1 tablespoon butter, for greasing

- ⅔ cup crumbled, drained feta cheese

- 3 fresh cilantro sprigs, to garnish

Baked Gnocchi in Tandoori Yogurt Sauce

1. Preheat the oven to 350°F and grease a casserole dish. Cook the gnocchi according to the package directions. Put the yogurt into a tall container and sprinkle it with the tandoori seasoning.

2. Add the lemon juice to the yogurt.

3. Season with salt and pepper.

4. Pour in the milk and stir well with a fork.

5. Arrange the gnocchi in the bottom of the prepared casserole dish and cover with the tandoori sauce.

6. Distribute the cheese evenly over the top.

7. Bake in the preheated oven for about 25 minutes, until the cheese is golden brown in color.

Serve straight from the casserole dish and garnish with cilantro sprigs.

■ Curry powder or garam masala can be used instead of tandoori seasoning.

*
* 35
*

10 ounces cooked polenta

 3 tablespoons olive oil, for greasing

10 ounces Gorgonzola cheese or other blue cheese

4 small tomatoes

salt and pepper, to taste

fresh oregano leaves, to garnish

Broiled Polenta with Tomatoes & Gorgonzola

1. Cut the polenta into 6 × 3-inch rectangles and brush both sides with oil. Preheat a ridged grill pan.

2. Put the polenta pieces into the pan and sauté on each side until golden.

3. Meanwhile cut the cheese into small pieces and the tomatoes into sixths.

4. Preheat the broiler to high. Grease a baking dish, then add the polenta slices in a single layer. Cover them with the tomatoes and pieces of cheese. Lightly season with salt and generously season with pepper. Place under the preheated broiler and cook for 3–5 minutes, until the cheese is melted.

Garnish with oregano and serve.

✳
✳
✳ 25

■ Cooked polenta is a dish made with an Italian-style cornmeal, available in Italian delicatessens and at specialty online stores. Broiled polenta is also delicious topped with lightly sautéed spinach and melted blue cheese, or broiled eggplant with a thick tomato sauce and mozzarella cheese.

2 yams

9 cups vegetable oil, for frying

salt, to taste

sugar, to taste

Homemade Yam Chips

1. Use a sharp knife to cut the skin from the yams.

2. Cut the yams into thin slices.

3. Lay the slices in cold water for 15 minutes to draw out the starches.

4. Place in a colander and rinse well under running water.

5. Dry the slices well in a dish towel.

6. Heat the oil in a deep saucepan to 340°F, add the yam slices, and sauté until crisp and golden brown.

7. Using a slotted spoon, remove the yam chips from the oil.

8. Spread the crisps in a single layer over paper towels to dry.

Sprinkle with salt or sugar, according to taste, and serve in bowls.

■ Serve the homemade yam chips with a light herb sauce or a piquant tomato salsa.

*
*
*
35

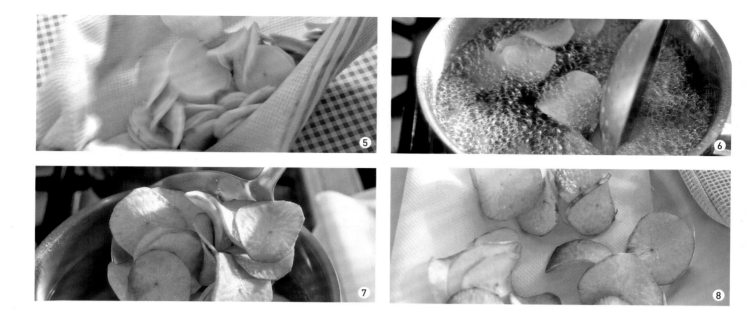

6–8 Yukon gold or russet potatoes, peeled

1 bunch fresh chives

1 egg

1 tablespoon sour cream or crème fraîche

pinch of freshly grated nutmeg

1 tablespoon butter

pinch of salt

⅓ cup cornstarch

⅓ cup all-purpose flour, for dusting

1 tablespoon vegetable oil, for greasing

Potato Cakes

1. Bring a large saucepan of lightly salted water to a boil, add the potatoes, bring back to a boil, and cook for 20 minutes, or until tender. Press the potatoes through a potato ricer.

2. Finely snip the chives and set aside. Form a little well in the center of the potatoes. Separate the egg and put the egg yolk, sour cream, nutmeg, chives, butter, salt, and cornstarch into the well.

3. Mix with your hands, and shape the mixture into an elongated roll. As you work, dust the roll with flour so that it doesn't stick to your hands.

4. Use a floured knife to slice the dough into ½-inch-thick circles.

5. Briefly toss the circles in flour and shape them into pattie shapes.

6. Grease a nonstick skillet, heat over medium heat, then add the potato cakes and cook for about 3 minutes on each side, until brown. Serve immediately.

■ Add crisp roasted cubes of ham to the potato mixture. Potato cakes go well with pork and veal dishes.

✳
✳✳ 45

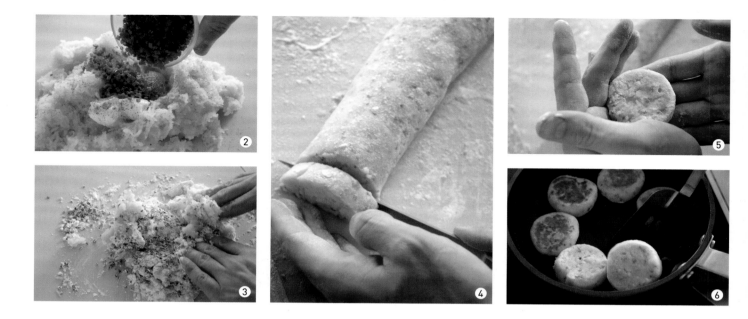

12 russet potatoes (about 3¼ pounds)

 12 cups vegetable oil

 1 teaspoon salt

French Fries

1. Peel the potatoes and cut into large wedges. Remove the corners in order to even out the sides. Cut the wedges into ½-inch-thick strips.

2. Wash thoroughly in cold water to remove the starch.

3. Dry the potato strips in a clean dish towel before deep-frying them. If the strips are damp, the oil will bubble up and splash.

4. Heat the oil in a large saucepan to 275°F. Add the potato strips and cook for about 1 minute without browning.

5. Remove the fries from the pan with a slotted spoon and let cool on a baking sheet.

6. Increase the temperature of the oil to 350°F, then return the fries to the pan and cook until they are crisp and golden.

7. Remove the fries from the oil and let drain on paper towels.

Season with salt and serve immediately.

■ In Belgium and France, fries are still traditionally deep-fried in beef suet or horse fat, then dried in preheated fabric napkins.

1 cup light cream

1 cup milk

salt and pepper, to taste

freshly grated nutmeg

2 garlic cloves, lightly crushed

8 white round potatoes, peeled

½ tablespoon butter, plus extra for greasing

Scalloped Potatoes

1. Preheat the fan oven to 375°F and lightly grease a casserole dish. Put the cream and milk in a saucepan and bring to a boil, then season with salt, pepper, and nutmeg. Add the garlic and let stand for 10 minutes, then pass the mixture through a fine strainer.

2. Cut the potatoes into very thin slices.

3. Layer the potatoes in the prepared casserole dish and pour the cream-and-milk mixture over the potatoes.

4. Dot the top evenly with butter.

5. Cover the dish with aluminum foil and use the tip of a knife to poke small holes in it. Bake in the preheated oven for about 20 minutes. Uncover the dish for the last 10 minutes of cooking, so that the dish cooks to a golden color.

Serve straight from the casserole dish.

✳✳✳ 40

■ You can also use Gruyère cheese or Swiss cheese in this dish. For a potato-and-leek casserole, gently sauté 2 sliced leeks in 1 tablespoon of butter. Grease the casserole dish and arrange the leeks on the bottom, then follow the instructions for the scalloped potatoes from Step 3.

1 garlic clove

1¼ pounds white round potatoes

1-inch piece fresh ginger

3 tablespoons vegetable oil

1 teaspoon fennel seeds

½ teaspoon ground turmeric

freshly grated nutmeg

salt, to taste

20 saffron threads

1¾ cups coconut milk

fresh mint leaves, to garnish

Indian Saffron Potatoes in Coconut Milk

1. Peel the garlic and finely chop. Peel the potatoes, cut them into 1¼-inch cubes, and place in cold water to prevent discoloration. Peel the ginger and cut into fine julienne strips. Heat the oil in a deep saucepan, add the garlic, ginger, fennel seeds, and turmeric, and gently sauté for 2–3 minutes.

2. Add the potato cubes, season with nutmeg and salt, and gently sauté for about 1 minute.

3. Add the saffron and gently sauté for a short time.

4. Pour in the coconut milk, cover the pan, and simmer for about 20 minutes. Stir occasionally and add some water, if necessary, so that the potatoes don't stick to the pan.

Arrange the potatoes in a bowl, sprinkle with mint leaves, and serve immediately.

■ You can also use garam masala instead of the various spices listed. Garam masala incorporates many flavors and is very versatile. Alternatively, half the potatoes can be replaced with cooked chickpeas. The addition of fresh scallions makes this variation especially delicious.

9 Yukon gold or russet potatoes

salt, to taste

1¼ sticks unsalted butter, chilled

1¼ cups milk

freshly grated nutmeg

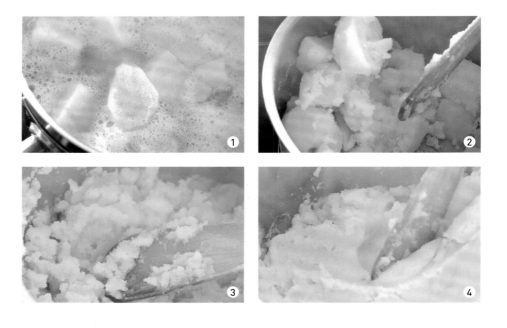

Homemade Mashed Potatoes

1. Peel and halve the potatoes. Bring a large saucepan of lightly salted water to a boil, add the potatoes, bring back to a boil, and cook for about 25 minutes, until the potatoes are tender.

2. Drain the potatoes and return them to the pan. Heat them on the stove for as long as it takes to boil away any remaining liquid and for the potatoes to become very floury.

3. Mash the potatoes with a wooden spoon or a potato masher.

4. Work the potatoes until you have a smooth texture.

5. Slice the butter, and work it into the potatoes.

6. The butter must be fully absorbed by the mashed potatoes.

7. Heat the milk, and gradually stir it into the mash.

8. Season with salt and nutmeg.

9. Use a wooden spoon to mix everything together. Do not use a wire whisk, because it will make the potatoes tough.

Transfer to a bowl and serve immediately.

■ Olive oil can be used instead of butter to smooth the mashed potatoes. However, be sure to use good-quality virgin olive oil.

* * * **40**

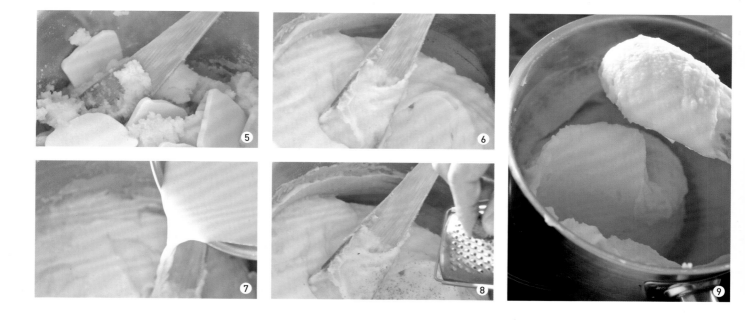

 1¼ pounds carrots

2 tablespoons butter

sugar, to taste

white pepper, to taste

1 cup Vichy mineral water

Vichy Carrots

1. Thinly slice the carrots.

2. Put the butter in a large saucepan and heat until foaming. Add the carrot slices, season with sugar and pepper, and lightly sauté. Add the mineral water, just covering the carrots in liquid, then bring to a boil.

3. Steam the carrots for approximately 10 minutes, covered, until almost all of the liquid has evaporated. Stir the carrots occasionally so that they cook evenly.

Transfer to a bowl and serve immediately.

* * * 25

■ In this recipe, Vichy mineral water is used as a substitute for salted water. If you like your carrots a little saltier, salt can be added to taste. It's important to use young carrots with green tops because they have a very delicate taste. Serve as an accompaniment to small veal cutlets or a roast.

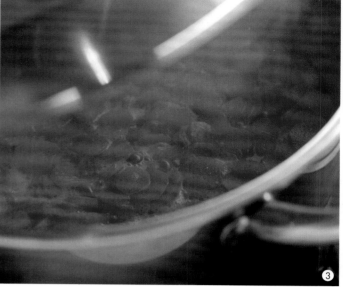

2 shallots

1 pound spinach leaves

3 tablespoons butter

salt and pepper, to taste

freshly grated nutmeg

1 garlic clove, peeled

Steamed Spinach Leaves

1. Finely dice the shallots. Wash the spinach leaves, drain, and remove the coarse stems. Melt the butter in a saucepan over medium heat, add the shallots, and sauté briefly.

2. Add the spinach leaves to the pan and season with salt, pepper, and nutmeg. Steam for about 3 minutes, until the liquid is reduced.

3. Spear the garlic with a fork and stir the spinach leaves with it, so that they acquire a subtle garlic flavor.

Serve the spinach leaves with roasted beef, broiled sole, or other saltwater fish.

30

■ To make creamed spinach, pour ½ cup light cream onto the uncooked spinach and let it reduce. Blend the cream and spinach with an immersion blender until smooth. Serve the creamed spinach as a side to a main meat dish, with pototoes, too.

2 ounces cooked ham

1 small onion

1 tablespoon butter

2 cups snow peas

3 cups peas

salt, to taste

sugar, to taste

white pepper, to taste

²⁄₃ cup chicken stock

½ head lettuce

2 fresh mint sprigs

1 tablespoon butter, chilled

Snow Peas Stewed with Lettuce & Ham

1. Cut the ham into thin strips. Finely dice the onion. Heat the butter in a large saucepan until foaming, add the ham and onion, and gently sauté.

2. Remove the snow pea stems and cut the pods diagonally twice. Add to the ham with the peas, mix together, and season with salt, sugar, and pepper.

3. Pour in the stock, cover the pan, and stew for approximately 5 minutes.

4. Cut the lettuce into strips. Finely chop the mint into strips. Add the lettuce and the mint to the peas, mix in the butter, and season with salt and pepper.

Serve immediately in individual bowls.

40

■ Fresh peas are the most delicious kind for this recipe. From 1 pound of pea pods, you should get about 1–1⅓ cups of unshelled peas. This dish is a good accompaniment to chicken.

2 shallots

1 bunch fresh parsley

1 garlic clove

4 cups shelled fava beans

3 tablespoons butter

salt and pepper, to taste

freshly grated nutmeg, to taste

Fava Beans with Garlic & Onions

1. Finely chop the shallots and parsley leaves. Peel the garlic and finely chop. Bring a saucepan of lightly salted water to a boil, add the beans, bring back to a boil and cook for 1 minute. Drain in a colander and rinse under cold running water.

2. Remove the white casing from the beans with your fingers. Very small beans can be cooked in their pods.

3. Put the butter in a skillet and heat until foaming, then add the shallots and garlic and gently sauté until they are translucent.

4. Add the beans and season with salt, pepper, and nutmeg.

5. Gently sauté for an additional 2–3 minutes, then add the parsley and mix.

Transfer the beans to bowls and serve.

■ For 4 cups of shelled beans, you will need approximately 6½ pounds unshelled fava beans. This dish can also be prepared using a combination of different beans. However, they should always be cooked in lightly salted water, until they are tender but still firm to the bite.